Endpapers: Well behaved Brown Burmese Kittens

HOWELL

Beginner's guide to

Burmese Cats

Gwen Jenkins and Rod U'ren

Editor
Dennis Kelsey-Wood

HOWELL BOOK HOUSE Inc.
230 Park Avenue
New York, N.Y. 10169

Library of Congress Cataloging-in-Publication Data

Jenkins, Gwen.
Howell beginner's guide to Burmese cats.

Summary: Discusses the history, care, breeding, and showing of Burmese cats.
1. Burmese cat. [1. Burmese cat. 2. Cats]
I. U'Ren, Rod. II. Kelsey-Wood, Dennis. III. Title.
SF449.B8J46 1986 636.8'25 86-20026
ISBN 0-87605-904-3

Photographic credits:

Printed in Australia by Fast Proof Press Pty. Ltd.

Contents

1. History

One would expect Burmese cats to have come from Burma, but this is not entirely the case. From all accounts of people who lived there, the brown Burmese were not typical cats of the country. The common cats were as varied in color as our own domestic cats, although different in type from European cats, and with a high incidence of kinks or change in angle of the vertebrae in the tail, especially near the tip.

The Brown Burmese is the original color and is still the most popular.

As far as one can ascertain, the Burmese that we know, all started with a little brown female cat called Wong Mau, who was taken from Burma to the United States of America in 1930 by Joseph C. Thompson, a retired ship's captain. Wong Mau was obviously of Malay type and American fanciers of the day regarded her as an especially dark Siamese.

Thompson, however, realized that she was differently marked from his Siamese and persuaded three breeders to co-operate with him in a series of breeding experiments intended to throw light on Wong Mau's genetic make-up.

The result of this was a paper published in the American Journal of Heredity in 1943. The investigation showed that Wong Mau was, in fact, a hybrid of Siamese with a new dark-coated breed of cat, which because of Wong Mau's origin, was called Burmese.

The breed was first recognized by the American registration bodies and later by the British Council of the Cat Fancy. These original Burmese cats were called sable in the U.S.A. and brown in Britain. Although the pure breed we have today was first isolated in the U.S.A., it is natural to wonder whether hybrids of Burmese crossed with Siamese, similar to Wong Mau, did not feature amongst the original Siamese imports into Britain around the turn of the century. It is inconceivable that Wong Mau was a unique cat, as it would be reasonable to deduce that inter-breeding of Burmese and Siamese was not uncommon in the Far East. If so, it would not be surprising to find some hybrids amongst early imports.

Burmese cats are now popular around the world and were introduced as far afield as Australia in 1957, with the importing of Tomahawk from the U.K. From the original brown, Burmese have been developed in many colors, and the breed is most popular at cat shows where it competes successfully with other foreign breeds.

2. Breed Description

Although the original Burmese were brown in color, some of these carried the blue factor (a paler gray tone) and when two of these were mated together they produced both brown and blue kittens. Additionally as Burmese became more popular, breeders successfully experimented with out-crossings to other breeds and from these we now have chocolate, lilac, red, cream, (blue tortoiseshell) and brown (seal) tortoise-shell.

The Burmese you see on the bench today is vastly different from the original Burmese/Siamese cross, as can be seen if we compare the standard, which is the officially accepted description of the breed, of the 1950's with that of the 1980's. The earlier standard called for a medium sized cat, dainty, long and elegant, with a long neck and slender legs proportionately slim, hind legs slightly higher than the front ones and feet small and oval in shape. The tail was to be long and tapering to a point, with only a slight kink at the extreme tip permissible. The head was to be long and pointed with relatively large pricked ears, yellow eyes, almond in shape and slanting towards the nose in true oriental fashion. The cat was to be in excellent physical condition, not fat, but inclined to muscle.

Bearing in mind that at this stage there were only brown Burmese, the body color in adult cats was to be a solid, rich, dark, seal brown and shading to slightly lighter on the chest and belly, with no white or tabby markings: the ears, mask (face) and points to be only slightly darker than the coat color of the back. The coat was to be glossy and short, fine in texture and lying close to the body.

Since then, the present day standard has been changed so the Burmese is an elegant cat of foreign type, which is positive and individual to the breed. Any suggestion of being either Siamese or solid and heavy like the British Shorthair is a fault. The body should be of medium length and size, feeling hard and muscular, heavier than its appearance indicates. The chest should be strong, the back straight from the shoulder to rump, legs slender and in proportion to the body; hind legs slightly longer than the front legs and paws neat and oval in shape. The tail is required to be straight and of medium length and not too heavy at the base, with a slight tapering to a rounded tip. A visible kink is a fault, but an invisible defect may be overlooked.

The head represents the main change in the standard. It should be slightly rounded on top with good width between the ears, having wide cheek bones, and tapering to a short blunt wedge with a firm chin, (the tapering created by the face narrowing towards the chin). The ears should be medium in size, as well as being set wide apart, with slightly rounded tips and their outer edge continuing the upper part of the head as seen from the front with a slightly forward tilt. A slight nose break (or indentation in the nose) is essential, and in profile the chin should show a strong lower jaw, not receding from the upper jaw. The eyes should be any shade of yellow, large and lustrous, neither rounded or oriental in shape, and set wide apart. The coat should be short and glossy of fine texture, and lying close to the body, which is indicative of good health. The cat should be well muscled, with a good weight for its size, and, particularly in kittens, lively and alert.

Left: This is an excellent head study of a Brown Burmese — showing the main change in the standard.

Below: The distinct gray tone of the Blue Burmese contrasts with the Brown Burmese.

3. Choosing a Kitten

For whatever reason, many people decide they want to own a Burmese; perhaps after reading this book, recommendation by a friend or having seen one somewhere. It must, then, be decided the purpose for which the kitten will be bought, as a pet, for breeding or for showing.

The description in the previous chapter refers to the standard required for show specimens, but many kittens will not come close to those requirements. Enough Burmese qualities will be there but to the connoisseur or the breeder, it will not come up to the show standard, and this is more than likely the main reason for it being sold as a pet. This should not matter for those wanting a pet, especially as there are other characteristics which are just as important, health, temperament and price, for example. More will be said later about identifying pets from breeding and show quality Burmese.

Alert Blue Burmese kittens.

Visiting the Breeder

Having answered an advertisement in a newspaper, contacted a registration council, or telephoned through someone recommending a particular breeder, you arrive at their home. Hopefully, the breeder will arrange for a number of kittens to make themselves known to you in the house. This will enable an unbiased decision to be made about whether the kitten is outgoing, runs about purring and is interested in visitors, or runs and hides under chairs; the latter being undesirable in the kitten's own environment.

One should not necessarily expect a breeder to take visitors into the cattery, not because there may be something to hide, but because cats, particularly young kittens, are very susceptible to diseases such as a range of cat flu type viruses, or feline infectious enteritis, or to such skin problems as ring-worm. It is unlikely that a visitor who does not have a cat already would be carrying such a health hazard on clothing, but due to the enormous cost such a problem might cause a breeder, most prefer not to take the risk.

On the other hand, it is quite reasonable to ask to see kittens at play as suggested above. Not being an expert, a potential buyer will not know all the finer points to look for, yet a few basics will enable the buyer to decide on the next most important characteristic, the general health of the kitten. A happy playful kitten is probably in good health anyway, showing an alert expression and clear lustrous eyes with no mucus coming from these or the nose. There should be no sores or fleas on the kitten's skin. It is useful to observe whether the kitten seems to have healthy teeth and gums, with a mouth free of tongue ulcers, although the breeder will not appreciate you forcing the mouth open to check, since it spreads infection.

If the kitten has been reared in the breeder's cattery, it may be a little nervous in the house, but it is still possible to tell whether it is used to being handled, fed well and groomed regularly.

A third factor you will need to know is whether the kitten is house-trained and, if so, to what. Some kittens may be trained to let their owner know when they want to go outside but normally, they are trained by their mother and/or their breeder to go to a tray, set in a predetermined place. The tray may contain one of a range of commercial litters, sawdust, sand or shredded newspaper. Various opinions exist about the preference of one of these over another. Some stick to the kitten's coat. others smell, or may be carried through the house.

Whichever method of training has been instituted, it is best to adhere to it for at least a short time after buying the kitten, as it is one less difference it has to adjust to when in its new home.

Immunization

Since cats are susceptible to a number of viruses and other illnesses, it is virtually mandatory that they be immunized against as many as possible. The normal injections are for feline enteritis and for the cat flu group of viruses. While both live and dead virus injections are obtainable, the dead virus is generally preferred, as there seems to be less likelihood of infection between injections or reaction after these. The most widely administered immunization is probably the FE-FR-FC (3-in-one) which gives immunity against panleucopenia, rhinotracheitis and calicivirus (all discussed in the next chapter). Two injections are given three weeks apart, after which full immunity is built up. It will not prevent all illnesses, as there are some for which no immunization is yet available.

The breeder should be asked if the kitten has been immunized and with what type of vaccine. In most cases, a veterinary certificate should be available to this effect.

When to take the kitten home

Most reputable breeders will not sell a pet kitten under about ten weeks of age and many will not do so until the kitten is twelve weeks. At the latter age a kitten is well developed, is eating extremely well and is old enough to have its permanent immunizations. Kittens at eight weeks old are losing immunity gained from their mother's milk, yet they are generally not considered old enough to be given even temporary injections. Vets will advise that immunizations given before the age of twelve weeks cannot be expected to provide full or lasting immunity as intended. However it is quite reasonable to visit and order a kitten which is younger than this, and in the best interests of both parties it is as well to pay the breeder a deposit on such a visit.

The kitten's diet

By the time a kitten is taken delivery of, it will probably be having four meals a day. Of these, two will be solid food and two a milk feed of some type. The breeder who is organized may be able to supply you with a printed diet chart, to be followed through the various stages of development of the new pet. If this is not available, you will at least be able to write down what the breeder recommends for a feeding schedule.

Three month old kittens will need the four meals daily, with a gradual decrease up to nine months in the number of meals, though the quantity, overall, will remain the same.

What to buy before the kitten comes home

Having decided upon which kitten is to be bought, certain equipment should be obtained. An enclosed carrying basket is a sound idea, as even a normally placid kitten may become upset at being taken by comparative strangers into a new environment. The carrying basket will be of invaluable assistance later on if the kitten should need to visit a veterinarian. A good pet shop will stock all items that will be required.

Other equipment to purchase before the kitten comes home should include a litter tray (about 15 cm (6 in) deep, so that the kitten can climb into it easily but is unable to kick litter all over the room) litter, grooming utensils (a soft brush and fine flea comb), a bed and bedding, food and water dishes (china or very smooth plastic ones are better, as the irritation of licking rougher dishes has been known to cause rodent ulcers on the lips) and finally and most importantly, food and dietary supplements. Too often, people buy a kitten on the spur of the moment and find themselves ill-prepared. Such a lack of materials is bound to make it difficult for the kitten to settle in quickly.

It is important, in the interests of the safety of both the cat and yourself, to always transport it in an enclosed carrying basket and never leave the animal loose in the car when you are travelling. This is vital when going to the vet's or to the family holiday home for the weekend, and so on. Never carry your cat into the vet's surgery in your arms or take it on a lead.

Taking delivery of your kitten

As the kitten is going to a new environment, it is in its best interests that this trauma be minimized. This is best done if all possible efforts are made to continue with some of the features of its former environment. These will be as follows:—

A detailed list of the diet that the kitten is used to, going as far as the exact type of meat and milk, prepared in the identical way, with the same supplements.

Meals at the same time of day.

The same kind of litter tray and contents and placed in a similar area of the house (if the kitten was reared in the house).

The same sort of bed and bedding.

A happy playful Brown Burmese kitten — a sign of good health.

A Tortie like this could produce a Cream like the one on the right of the photo.

One would choose either of these kittens for their outgoing natures, in preference to kittens who tend to hide.

Kittens are normally trained by their mother to go to a litter tray set in a predetermined place.

Arrival home should be done without a lot of noise, which may frighten the kitten. The first thing to do is show it where its litter tray is, putting it in the tray a couple of times to reinforce the point. Over the next couple of days, whenever it seems to be scratching for corners, or is uneasy, looking for somewhere to hide or is crying out, it may be an indication that it wants to use its tray. In case it has become disoriented in its new surroundings, carry the kitten to the tray and place it in again. Most kittens accept this situation quickly.

If the kitten comes out of the carrying basket purring, there will most likely not be any difficulties in its settling in. This is quite natural and in any case it is to be expected that the kitten will walk around sniffing much of what it sees. It may be advisable to limit the kitten to a couple of rooms for the first day or so, and gradually expand this area as curiosity gets the better of your pet.

The kitten which hides under beds and refrigerators will need to be limited to just one room until it feels more at ease. For the nervous kitten, it is especially important to ensure that it knows where its tray is and has full access to it. It is this kitten which is most likely to have a stomach upset and consequently have most need of its tray.

Toilet trays should be placed strategically around the house, for example in the bathroom, laundry and in a corner, so there is no excuse for an accident.

As soon as the kitten has had a look around, and been made to feel at home, it is a good idea to offer it some food or milk, as such action establishes the new owner as the person to be relied upon for nourishment, and helps the kitten to feel more secure. If your household has small children, it is important that they do not have free access to the kitten, being allowed to handle it only under supervision while it is settling in.

Once food has been offered, the new bed should then be produced. As much time as possible should be spent with the kitten, as this has the effect of bringing it out of its shell, especially if it is nervous, and will also familiarize the animal with its new family. Even some rolled up paper, an open supermarket shopping bag or a small ball will pay enormous dividends at this stage.

Having taken the preceding introductory steps, it is reasonable to expect, that within a few days, the kitten will be playing and eating well. The start of a long and rewarding partnership has begun.

Living arrangments.

From experience as a breeder of these cats, it seems that when a Burmese kitten joins a household, it is important to realise that it will expect to be one of the family, that is, to eat and sleep with one. It may desire to use the special basket with down cushion, or the bean bag that you purchased from the pet shop, just on odd occasions, but most times it will be either sleeping in your arms, after much scrabbling to get there, on your chest or, in hot weather, on your head, and there is not much to be done about it.

If one should try to shut it out, in its basket and corner, one will be kept awake with much crying and then deadly silence, so that one may start to wonder if it has choked itself or has suffocated. On investigation, a bundle of fur launches itself into one's arms. The result is that the kitten finishes up on the bed after all.

Burmese do love a romp in the garden if possible, but human companionship is the most essential thing for this particular breed and you should only acquire one if you are prepared to devote long periods to the company of your pet.

Grooming

One of the advantages of owning a Burmese is that very little grooming is required. However a short list of easy activities to help in the general comfort and appearance of your cat is given in order that it can be kept — and look — in the very best of health.

Ears. The cat's ears should be checked at least weekly for any evidence of ear-mite or wax build-up. An oily or even black discharge will emerge from the ears if there is a problem, though regular checking will always prevent such a condition from ever developing. Routine action may include wiping out the ear gently with a cotton ball moistened with a safe light oil such as baby oil.

Fleas. The Burmese need to be checked regularly for fleas by combing them systematically with a fine, round-tipped flea comb. Under normal conditions, this should be done weekly, though when the weather is dry for prolonged periods, a flea plague may require more frequent care. In such times, a good flea powder may be used, especially if the area is sandy or if cats roam free a great deal. In extreme cases, it may be beneficial to bath the cat in a medicated shampoo. Then pour a very diluted solution of a cat type malathion solution over the animal and towel it dry without washing the malathion off, following the manufacturer's directions to the letter, and taking great care not to allow any of the solution to go into the cat's eyes.

Grass seeds and burrs. Where Burmese roam fairly freely, as they like to do if given the chance, it is also wise to check regularly for grass seeds or burrs in their ears, between their paw pads and under the front legs, as these can cause severe irritation and may become infected if left untreated.

General grooming. After the foregoing have been attended to, one may brush a small quantity of baby powder through the coat. A chamois rubbed down over the coat and a final wipe over with a piece of silk will help give the characteristic Burmese shine.

4. The Health of your Burmese

The well-being of the Burmese can be grouped in many ways, with one possible method being into visible and internal difficulties. While a veterinarian will be able to give much more detail and is trained in the treatment of our pets, there are many things the Burmese owner can learn to look for. Some of the more obvious of these are listed below, with treatment which has been found to help. Remember, if in doubt, it always pays to consult a veterinarian.

The ideal time to mate a Burmese is from nine months of age like this Brown kitten.

Visible Problems

External Parasites: Fleas and mites are the most usual pests in this category. Fleas may be seen on the skin and blood staining may appear in the coat. Mites cause distressful, itchy patches on the skin. Both conditions are treated by first washing the cat in medicated shampoo and then, for fleas, applying a 1:70 solution or for mite a 1:35 solution of cat formula malathion.

Eczema: Dry or running sores on the skin may indicate this condition which may be caused by a number of factors. Consult veterinarian.

Running Eyes: Will cause staining down face. Wipe eyes with tissue once or twice daily. A weak solution of boracic acid can be used to wash eyes and stained area. Consult veterinarian if symptoms persist.

Mucus in Nose: Will cause cat to sneeze often and violently. Could be related to cat 'flu' virus. Consult veterinarian.

Ear Mite: Blackish wax in ears and dark staining around ears, cat will scratch often. A contagious condition which requires urgent treatment. Consult veterinarian.

Stud Chin and Stud Tail: Consists of pimples and black heads on infected area. Easy to squeeze out and wash the infected area with medicated shampoo. Check regularly for control.

Diarrhea: Will cause staining down the back legs. Often the symptom of another disease. Reduced canned milk and meat and consult veterinarian.

Cream Burmese originally sprung from breeding a Blue Burmese with a tabby.

5. Colors of Burmese

Before deciding on the color of your Burmese, it is useful to visit a show in your vicinity. For information on such shows, contact the registration body of felines in your area.

Readers will note that a general description of the Burmese has already been given in Ch. 2. A more specific version, based on the American standard, is now inserted to help new breeders decide on the type of cat they purchase.

Standard for all colors

General:	Ideally, the Burmese is a medium sized cat, solid in bone, muscular and heavier than appearances indicate. It shows no sign of being fat, alert and has an expressive face.
Head:	Rounded front-on or side-on. The face is full, broad and tapering to a short muzzle. The nose has a distinct break or dent between the eyes.
Ears:	Medium, well apart on a rounded head, rounded on the tips and broad at the base.
Eyes:	Set well apart, rounded. In the U.K. and Australia, more specific detail asks for the eyes also to be rounded in the lower line, but with the upper outline straighter and slanting slightly towards the nose. Round or oriental eyes are a fault.
Body:	Medium, muscular and compact, with back level and chest rounded. Males are a little larger than females.
Legs:	In proportion to the body.
Paws:	Round. 5 toes on front feet, 4 on back feet.
Tail:	Straight, medium length. Some standards state that it should not be tapering.
Coat:	Short, lying close to the body, fine and glossy. The satin finish indicates good health.
Color:	Large range, but the underparts will be slightly lighter than the back.
Nose Leather & Paw Pads:	According to coat color (details given under each coat color).

Eye Color: Yellow to gold. In some countries, chartreuse is allowed; a color more likely to be evident in Blue or Lilac Burmese, sometimes Reds.

Faults: These include kink in tail, green or blue eyes, lockets or other white spots, incorrect number of toes. These faults are penalised to different degrees according to country or region.

The above standard applies to all colors of Burmese. Individual differences in various colors are given in the following pages and this section is more aligned with standards other than the American one.

Brown Burmese:

The original and still the most popular Burmese is the Brown, sometimes called Seal. It has a dark, glossy, brown coat and has a rich, warm look, which is usually slightly darker on the face and ears (collectively called the mask), shading to slightly lighter on the underparts.

In practice, the more even the color over the entire cat the better, and it should not be too dark, with no hint of being black. Even in the Browns, it is not uncommon to see a small patch of white hairs on the neck, stomach or groin and care should be taken not to breed with such cats and to penalise them on the show bench.

Nose Leather & Paw Pads should be rich or dark brown to complement the coat color. The golden eyes stand out very clearly against this uniformly dark color.

Blue Burmese:

It is generally thought that the Blue Burmese were the products of hybrid stock or Burmese/Siamese mixture. The term "blue" in the context of shorthair breeds refers to shades of gray, which are a cold tone similar to the color of the points of the Blue Point Siamese. According to the standard, the Blue Burmese adult is a soft, silver gray, with a silver sheen on the rounded parts. Like the Brown, the mask of the Blue will be slightly darker and the underparts a little lighter, though a little less apparently so than the Browns.

Eye color should be yellow, but it is hard to obtain the richer, golden color of the Brown Burmese in the Blues, with the result that these tend to have a less intense tone.

Nose Leather & Paw Pads are to be gray and dark gray respectively, to match the coat color.

The above two colors are more established than the rest. Chocolates through to Creams are newer, with the Tortoiseshell group being a little newer again and at the time of writing appear not to be on Challenge status in all countries.

The Brown Burmese has a dark and glossy brown coat.

Blue Burmese are a cold gray tone similar to the color of the Blue Point Siamese.

The Lilac Burmese has a pale, delicate, warm, dove gray coat with a slightly pinkish tone.

In the absence of a Red or Cream Burmese, a Tortoiseshell is needed to breed this Red Burmese.

Chocolate Burmese:

As far as one can ascertain, the Chocolate and Lilac Burmese began in the U.S.A., were imported into the U.K., and then spread to the rest of the world in a variety of ways. The Chocolate only appeared in the late 1960's, so it is still a fairly new color and as such is quite uncommon in some areas. When one considers that the first pedigreed Persians were bred in the 1860's, the lack of numbers is easily understood perhaps.

The Chocolate is reported to have been bred from a chocolate male and female on the east coast of the U.S. and from a brown male and female, both carrying the new chocolate gene, on the west coast of the country. From this basic stock, it is presumed that the lilac-colored (pale-colored equivalent) Burmese were bred in the U.K., as in the early 1970's Lilac Burmese were bred in Britain from cats with both the chocolate gene and the dilute (pale) gene.

The Chocolate Burmese should have an even milk chocolate coat, though unfortunately this is rarely seen. Most standards say that the even color is desirable, but slight variations of color on the points (mask, legs, feet and tail) are permitted. In practice, large variations often still exist.

Eye color should still be any shade of yellow and it is normally quite good.

Nose Leather is to be warm chocolate brown. **Paw Pads** are a brick pink shading to chocolate.

Lilac Burmese:

The coat color should be a pale, delicate, warm, dove gray, with a slightly pinkish tone, giving a rather faded effect. As with the Chocolates, the mask and other points tend to be slightly darker than the body, though less than in the darker Chocolates. In the same way as the Blues compared with the Browns, this lesser difference is to be expected, as the two lighter coats have less scope for variation. Even so, the mask may be slightly darker than the rest of the coat.

As in any breed of cat, lilac is a most exacting color, with lack of warmth or too much warmth being an important quality; a characteristic relating to the amount and quality of chocolate showing in the coat.

Eye color is required to be yellow still, though as with the Blues it is difficult to breed the richer yellow of the Browns.

Nose Leather is lavender pink and **Paw Pads** are similar in adults.

Red & Cream: Red and Cream Burmese seem to have sprung from a breeding program begun accidentally in the U.K. In 1965, when a Blue Burmese escaped and mated with a local shorthaired tabby, from which was produced a Tortoiseshell of foreign type.

At this stage, it is important to understand a little basic genetics. The red (or cream) color of any cat is inherited via the same chromosome (the microscopic strand of information by which inherited qualities are passed on) as the one which determines the sex of the cat. Space does not allow for its discussion in this book, but readers should be aware of its existence. However, it must be understood that, in the absence of a red or cream cat, the new breeder needs a tortoiseshell to breed Red or Cream Burmese.

Clearly, because of the possibility of variation on one cat, both nose leather and paw pads may be a plain color or blotched.

Scale of Points for Burmese

All cats, including Burmese, are judged on a scale of points out of 100. While the allocation of these points varies from country to country and from one registration body to another, sometimes even within a country or part of a country, the following gives some idea of the relative importance of the features of the Burmese:—

Head	-20 -25 points
Shape and set of eyes	-5 -15 points
Body, legs and tail	-25 -30 points
Eye color	-5 -30 points
Coat color & condition	-25 -40 points

The variations above reflect the different importance various bodies place on the different aspects of the cat. In the Tortoiseshells, even fewer points may be allocated for the coat and color due to the often acknowledged difficulty in controlling the arrangement of color, as indicated earlier in this chapter. The effect for them is to give more points to type.

Judging a Brown Tortoiseshell on color is very difficult so more points are usually allocated to type.

Although the nose leather & paw pads arè a plain color in these Red and Cream Burmese, they may be blotched.

6. Breeding — A Guide to Breeding Colors

The person who buys a Burmese for a pet may never intend to breed cats. Nevertheless, new breeders are constantly joining clubs and they are nearly always people who have a desexed pet and want to go further.

Breeding is a serious business and needs to be proceeded with considerable caution. Calling females, helping at birth and all the work of rearing kittens must be allowed for. It is vital also to avoid breeding with inferior stock.

Choosing a Female

Though there is a degree of luck in breeding, inferior females are likely to produce only more of the same. The lesson is "buy the best available right from the start". It will cost more, but will save time and money overall.

The Female in Season

There is no doubt when a female cat is in season; breeders say she is "calling". Females react in different ways. They may go off their food and slink around the house, crouching frequently with the rump in the air and treading the back legs, howling in a strange manner and wanting to escape from their pen. Quieter females may be more secretive.

This behavior continues for three to seven days, with a break of about six weeks before another round. However, as little as two weeks may be the pattern for a particular female.

When to Mate the Female Burmese

Burmese are rather precocious and can often come into their first season as early as five months. This first season tends to be a rather half-hearted affair, but do not ignore the effort, as given the opportunity the Burmese female will mate anyway.

The ideal time to mate a Burmese is from about nine months of age, so allowing for a gestation of 63 to 65 days (often a day or two longer) the cat would be about eleven months when the kittens are born.

Some quick arithmetic shows that early callers may well have had four or five calls by ten months. This creates the next problem as it is ideal to mate her on her second call (some variation of opinion exists here). Most cats have their first litter according to the book; the others create the problem. Sometimes, a female which called early and continues to call regularly, has to be mated younger than one would like, with the hope that she has developed physically and emotionally well enough to cope with rearing a family.

The alternative is to let her have more than two or three calls before mating. In nature, animals mate when in season, but it is worth remembering we are dealing with a manufactured breed. Consequently, waiting one more call with such females may produce cystic ovaries, resulting in difficulty on conceiving later. Before this happens, the female will tend to call continually without a break in between calls. If she gets to this stage, she clearly has to be mated whether she seems large enough or not. Fortunately, more desperate and closer calls give warning of this state.

Some breeders and veterinarians may suggest putting the female on the pill, involving a small dose of a tablet, commonly ovarid. Whilst this treatment certainly prevents "calling", experience shows that many cats so treated have difficulty conceiving afterwards and a few take twelve months to do so. Some have been known never to conceive.

The other factor to consider is the female's general health and condition. There are a few basics to investigate: visible signs like fleas, mite, worms, ring-worm or ear mite, a healthy coat and bright expressive eyes. Any sign of viruses or illness of any kind should also be cleared up, as the female cannot be expected to produce a healthy litter if she is under undue stress.

Since some conditions cause kittens not to be conceived, carried full-term, not to develop correctly or survive after birth, it is always advisable to make sure females are fully immunised and appear in top health.

Choice of Stud

The first ground rule is "the stud contributes only half the qualities of the kittens", the female contributes equally. The second rule is to "choose the stud carefully". At the start, one has to decide what color or group of colors is to be bred and acquire a female to this end, trying to make up one's mind from the many different opinions, verbal and written, what is the best-way to breed the chosen color. The stud is chosen on the basis of the following:—

(a) He will help produce the colors desired.
(b) He has excellent type.
(c) His pedigree indicates he should produce excellent kittens.
(d) His pedigree has some linkages with the female's pedigree.
(e) He is available for stud service to the female concerned.
(f) He is not being used because of cheapness.
(g) He is not being used because he belongs to a friend.

It may be of help to remember that a maiden female (having her first litter) needs the easiest time possible for her. Also, as stated earlier, the best pair of cats can produce inferior kittens and one should not necessarily expect a female to have top quality kittens even when bred with the best stud available.

It is advisable that the maiden queen is sent to a suitable stud close to home. She should not be sent interstate or too far away for her first mating, even to choose a special pedigree until she is a proven breeder.

Stud Fees

There is no regulation which sets how much a stud fee should be. It is completely a personally based figure, decided on such things as those which decide kitten prices, plus how widely the stud is used, and limitations placed on his offspring and perhaps the owner's interest in stud work. As a general rule, the higher the stud fee, the better the stud cat or the better his potential. Of course, this does not always follow. The top stud male may be totally unrelated to the female and the kittens poor quality. Better kittens could result from a lesser male which is partly related, having one or two excellent cats on both pedigrees. The deciding factor may be how much one can afford to pay for a stud fee and to work within this limitation.

A final factor may be that the stud owner offers a free stud fee in exchange for a kitten from the proposed mating. This avoids the owner of the female parting with direct cash; sometimes an attractive offer.

Mating the Female

Having arranged before the female comes onto call to take her to the stud of your choice, the next step is to contact the stud owner as soon as the female starts to come into season, to get full benefit of the call and ensure she will conceive. Some females conceive at different times during the call, so it is best for her to be there as long as possible during the call.

It is normal for the female to go off call temporarily for a day or two when she visits the stud, due to the new surroundings. She will also normally stop eating for a while, for the same reason.

Ideally, your female is placed in a pen next to the stud in question and where she cannot see any other stud. If she is one of the placid ones which does not go off call on arrival and spit at the stud, she may be placed in with him the day of arrival. More commonly, this occurs some time in the first forty-eight hours. Once she is strongly calling, she will encourage the stud to approach her and he will be able to mate her easily.

The actual mating may take from only a couple of minutes up to a slow, frustrating half hour or more. The female gives a high-pitched scream when penetration occurs, followed by a somewhat violent rolling and thrashing from side to side. The male jumps clear, up to a safe distance on a bench above her if he can. Both cats proceed to wash themselves energetically once this frenzy is completed. Mating may be repeated within ten minutes or so if the female is left with the stud, though it is better practice for her to be removed back to her own pen for an hour or so if she is a visitor, to give both cats a rest.

When the female is nervous or uncooperative, it is better to wait longer and let her settle in, talking to her and handling her often. She can be introduced to the stud a few times a day, but it is important to stay with her to monitor her reactions and encourage her as the stud makes efforts to approach her. If she remains timid despite calling, results may be obtained by backing her into the stud's pen, all the while holding her firmly by the back of the neck with one hand, so she may not notice when the stud mounts and also takes her by the back of the neck. By constantly talking to her, it is often possible for mating to be completed by this subterfuge.

The female is best mated at least three times, over 24 to 36 hours, whilst some may mate much more. Tense cats are likely to have more difficulty in conceiving, perhaps needing a larger number of matings. Maiden queens, likewise, are usually much less cooperative, being both more difficult to mate, more nervous and more likely not to conceive on the first visit. Further, they may not like the particular stud chosen for them, thus interfering with plans.

Two playful kittens in a kitchen.

The Chocolate Tortoiseshell is a fairly new color.

A Brown Burmese tending to her kitten.

How Will the Owner of the Stud Cat Help You?

There are several things one might expect to be done to assist the breeder, in particular the new and inexperienced breeder:—

(a) The stud fee and any other costs will be set before the visit.
(b) What colors are possible from the planned mating will be discussed.
(c) Any restrictions on how the owner of the female may dispose of the kittens will be discussed before the visit.
(d) Most stud owners will accept a return mating if the female does not conceive, but this is at the discretion of the stud owner and not a right. This should also be checked before the visit.

Is She Pregnant?

A maiden queen will show visible signs of pregnancy at 3 weeks after the mating. However, the first signs are likely to be an increase in appetite from 2 to 2½ weeks on, together with the possibility of an improvement or decline in her manner towards people. At 3 weeks, her nipples will start to become pink, together with a crustiness of them and the area around them. The nipples may show a slight increase in size. A pinking of the nipples without crustiness usually means she has not conceived and is about to call again. For the last week, she will want to scratch in dark corners, turning over bedding and shredding any paper she can find. This is making a nest for her young.

Assuming the female does conceive, she will need extra care, entailing more food than previously and extra calcium and vitamin supplements, as her system will be draining these from her to the developing kittens. If she is a poor eater normally, she may naturally eat more during pregnancy: if not, a supplement with a yeast flavour will often persuade her to eat more anyway.

An experienced breeding queen will often develop the symptoms described as early as 2½ weeks, though breeders should not expect this.

At about 4 weeks, the female will become rounder and fuller; a process which continues at different external rates, depending on how the kittens lie inside. By 5 or 6 weeks, she tends to become less active and will experience discomfort from 6 weeks onwards that may make her even more inclined just to sit around and walk only short distances before resting. This will be much more obvious if the litter is going to be large.

In the last few days, a little light pink discharge may emerge from the vagina, in a mucus-like form. This should not be the cause for any concern. About 24 to 36 hours before birth, though, there are variations in this pattern, the milk will start to fill up the mammary glands so that they hang down a little under the cat. The kittens, instead of sitting out to the sides of the female, will drop back and underneath, giving a flatter shape than the mother has had for a week or two. The kittens are getting ready to enter the birth canal and be born. About 12 hours before she gives birth, the female's temperature drops. This can be measured with a thermometer, though a little experience will enable the breeder to feel that the ears have become colder. In line with this change, the cat usually declines food.

The mother spends most of her time where the kittens will be born and will more than likely want a person or another cat to keep her constant company. Some have been known to hold off birth until company arrives.

Problems During Pregnancy

Most females proceed through their pregnancy without any problems. There are a few things which may worry the breeder. The most likely of these are:—

(a) Lack of eating. More variety in diet or supplements such as yeast often help.

(b) Lack of filling-out despite confirmed pregnancy. There may be only one or two kittens or perhaps some of the litter is reabsorbed.

(c) Lack of energy and an anaemic appearance. Some females have morning sickness, some may not handle pregnancy well or there may be something amiss with the developing kittens. The mother may have a problem such as leukaemia, which drains her energy. Seek professional help if this is a worry.

(d) Discharge during pregnancy. Some or all of the litter may be aborted. Thunder, major stress, falling with a twist or landing heavily after a jump may cause this. It is usually too late to prevent the abortion once there are visible signs. It is better to let nature take its course in most cases, find out whatever the problem was if possible, treat it, then try again for a full-term litter with clinical guidance, which may include holding shots or hormone implants to encourage full-term pregnancy. Not all vets like such treatment.

(e) Failure to call again despite lack of confirmed pregnancy. There may be what is called a phantom — or pseudo-pregnancy, in which the female develops pink nipples and swells up as if pregnant, though she does not have any kittens. Then one normally has to wait until about the seventh week for the cat to call. A course of anti-biotics followed by waiting for the following call until the cat is re-mated is normal procedure.

(f) Early birth or birth of some partly-developed kittens. Depending on the stage of pregnancy, miniature foetuses or virtually fully-formed kittens, with or without fur, may be seen. Often the mothers eat the evidence, perhaps not quite realising what it is. Even if only a few days early, kittens may not survive more than a day or so after birth.

It has been known for females to bite the heads off all kittens. If this happens with your queen, have her checked by the veterinarian and take his or her advice as to whether she should be bred with. It may be better to cut your losses from the start, have her spayed and try again with another breeding female. If in doubt with such a female, consult the breeder or a vet.

There may be other causes of the above problems. Those discussed are from the experience of the writers and other breeders and the causes and solutions are given within that framework.

Burmese have four to eight kittens, like this Cream.

Birth of Kittens

The section "Is She Pregnant" dealt with the stages of development before birth, at the end of which the female is about to deliver. A general description of what may be expected at birth now follows.

The cat is very restless, because she is uncomfortable, and she is waiting for the delivery to start. She may stretch out a few times, an action which should not be confused with contractions. These latter are easily recognisable from the back feet being stretched out behind her as the stomach depresses inwards and towards the rear. To begin with, the contractions may occur singly and be as much as twenty minutes apart. As labour progresses, they become closer and in clearer groups; perhaps three or four at a time and about two or three minutes apart, after anything from fifteen minutes to an hour or more. Variations from one female to another are great in both timing and number of contractions.

During this stage, it is normal for a discharge of light pink mucus to emerge from the vagina. After a while, this will increase in quantity and a small sack will appear, which in turn breaks; a process which is termed "the breaking of the water". The quantity of fluid varies greatly.

The closely-spaced contractions may continue for ten to thirty minutes before the first kitten is visible in the now distended vagina. Kittens may present head-first or feet-first, with 50% either way expected. More difficult presentations are fortunately rare, with veterinary assistance being needed when they occur (recognised perhaps by the failure of a kitten to proceed further). In any case, once the head emerges, the rest of the kitten normally follows with the next group of two contractions. If there is any delay, it sometimes helps to break the sack over the nose so that the kitten can start breathing, as many kittens die at birth or soon after from suffocating or drowning in their sack, or from pneumonia which develops from liquid associated with the slow delivery. It is also common for the mother to scream, sometimes profusely, during the birth, so unless this is prolonged, one need not worry.

It is quite normal for the female to eat the afterbirth of her kittens. She does this instinctively so as not to leave any evidence for predators, as they may also be attracted to the kittens.

If the mother is slow to attend to the new kitten, it may save problems to wipe the sack from the kitten's face, again to help clear its airways. The sudden eruption of the kitten during birth may well attend to this, forcing the kitten out of the sack. The afterbirth, a flat piece of tissue of a rich, red color, will be attached to the kitten's stomach via the umbilical cord, commonly about 15 centimetres (6 inches) long. If the kitten has emerged, but not the afterbirth, it may be possible to gently ease it out of the mother if she contracts further. Equally likely is that the cord will break, leaving the after-birth in the birth canal. It will be discharged later, normally before the next kitten.

If the kitten is slow to breathe and/or the mother remains slow to react to the situation, a number of steps may be taken:—

(a) Clear the face entirely with a tissue.

(b) Clear the body quickly with a tissue so the kitten can be handled without slipping out of one's hands.

(c) Take the umbilical cord between the index finger and thumb of each hand about five centimetres (two inches) from the kitten's body and tear through the cord with the nails. If the cord bleeds badly, clamp it for a couple of minutes with sterliised tweezers or similar instrument or hold between finger and thumb. Never cut the cord with a knife or scissors, as such a clear break may encourage bleeding.

(d) If the kitten is crying loudly and clearly, all is probably well. If there is no cry or a soft one, muffled by fluid in the trachea, pick the kitten up by the tail and back legs and strip down the body slowly and not too hard with the forefinger and thumb, as if milking a cow, all the while taking great care not to drop the wet and possibly still slippery kitten. Fluid will come out of the nostrils and mouth. Wipe this off with a tissue and repeat the process a few times until no more fluid emerges. The kitten's voice will become louder and clearer and the kitten more lively.

Where the kitten is presented tail-first, the birth is slower and more likely to require assistance. It may be born naturally, but if only the tail is emerging with contractions then withdrawing in between, it may be possible to hold the tail whilst protruding until the next contractions, then hold the feet as they appear. The kitten should gradually be born, especially as one is able to gain a firmer grip on the body.

In such births, the kitten is normally trying to breathe before it is born, so Step "d" may be more important here. Tail-first kittens often have swollen back legs as a result of the blood supply being temporarily cut off. This may impede their movement in feeding for a couple of days, but it normally goes down after this time. Of more concern are kittens whose heads are delivered but whose shoulders are stuck. Here, the head swells up and the kitten has difficulty feeding for the first day or so due to the pain. Such kittens may die through starvation.

In addition, all afterbirths need to be accounted for. The mother will eat a number of them, as suggested earlier, but any left in the uterus can cause rapid infection. An oxytocin injection within 24 hours of birth is a sensible practice in this regard.

It will be obvious when the mother has finished giving birth, as she will wash the kittens a little, settle down, go to sleep and allow the kittens to feed. A drink of diluted evaporated milk with half a teaspoon of glucose powder will help her settle and give her energy. The kittens should be eager to nose about for nipples for a drink.

Birth problems are mostly few. Normally, a trip to the veterinarian will be suggested if the cat is contracting strongly for some hours and getting nowhere. Such problems are outside the scope and space of this book and one should always seek professional help if in doubt.

To Rear Burmese Kittens

Much of what needs to be said on rearing a kitten is described in Ch. 3 in the section "The Kitten's Diet": this applying to a kitten 3 months or more. This chapter now applies to people rearing their first litter before that age and wondering if they are doing the best for the kittens.

Before the Kittens Eat for Themselves

The kittens have been fed from the day they were conceived, through the way in which their mother has been cared for. As soon as they are born, the mother will need more food than before the birth, apart from the first day or even two days. Quite commonly, the mother will eat nothing or very little at this time, prefering just to drink milk or not even that. She may choose to rest; many new mothers choosing not to move out of the box their kittens are in for up to three days, to the point of not using their bowels or bladder. As long as they seem in good health and the kittens are warm and quiet, sleeping in a heap, there is usually no cause for alarm at this lack of activity.

For the first twenty-four hours or so, the mother's milk consists of colostrum, an almost clear liquid which is rich in antibodies and therefore helps give the kittens immunity. After this, the normal milk is produced, evidenced by the much greater volume of the mammary glands, particularly the rear ones.

The eyes will open in from four to seven days, though some greater variation is known to occur. If the eyes are open at birth, though, veterinary help should be sought. All kitten's eyes are blue at first and turn slowly from about four weeks onwards to whatever color they will be in the adult cat; taking many months.

Weaning

From birth up to about 3 weeks the kittens rely on their mother for sustenance. From this age on, the kittens could become interested in their mother's meat. Also, depending on how forward they are, their noses may be dipped in a saucer of evaporated milk (half water) and baby cereal. If they are doing extremely well on their mother, this step may be held off for a week or so, but they tend to grow better once they have the double source of food. There is no cause for alarm if one or two kittens in a litter refuse to feed from a saucer until a week or two later.

Kittens a week or two older should be introduced to finely-scraped beef if they have not already begun stealing from their mother's dish. Tinned baby food on a saucer will also often entice them. Eating at this stage is often quite a messy business and it is often necessary to place food in the kitten's mouths for them to get the taste of it before they will eat. Those ready for solid food frequently wolf their meat as if ravenous and growl strongly at anything which comes near as they eat.

Kittens bought as pets, will be cheaper than if sold for showing or breeding.

Healthy Burmese are lively and alert, like these "athletes".

Large variations in color exist in the Chocolate and Tortoiseshell Burmese.

A Guide to Breeding

If you have made up your mind to breed Burmese, it is advisable to start with one color, preferably one which will produce a limited number of colors. The Brown or Blue would be a good choice, as the likelihood of a large range of colors is much reduced if bred with carefully. Then, once a year or two's experience has been gained, the newer breeder may then want to experiment with some of the other Burmese colors.

The inheritance of colors in any breed of cats is one of the more complex aspects of breeding and one needs a certain amount of basic knowledge about what colors can be produced from planned matings.

The first step is to learn the difference between "pure" colors and the "carrying" of colors. "Pure" means that a cat has in its genetic make-up two genes for a particular color and that in most circumstances it will produce only what is visible on the coat. e.g. Pure Brown mated to Pure Brown will produce only 100% Brown Burmese. If one mates such a cat to a Tortoiseshell, then the story becomes more complex, but this is outside the beginner's group of colors recommended above.

At the same time, a cat can "carry" a single gene for another color, which will show up in the offspring when the cat is mated to another cat carrying the same color gene. e.g. Brown carrying (c.) the dilute (blue) gene mated to another Brown cat c. dilute will produce both Brown and Blue offspring.

Clearly, "pure" means having two genes for a color; "carrying" means having only one gene for a color. Colors which are carried are really more involved than this and breeders who are interested in following this up should consult a more detailed text on cat genetics, especially one which explains recessive genes.

Very briefly, a recessive gene is one which has to be inherited from both parents before it can be visible in offspring. It may be the dilute gene carried by a Brown which could produced a Blue if mated to another cat of the same genetic make-up or to a Blue. The chocolate gene also is a recessive gene which can be carried by many colors, e.g. by brown, blue, red or cream. In any case, two of the same gene are required before the recessive gene can be seen on the cat, and as stated above, one of these has to be inherited from each parent.

A gene which is carried, by definition, is a recessive gene.

Below is a simplified color mating list, which gives the principal matings and expected kitten colors for the group of which the Brown and Blue Burmese are a part.

Symbols Used:	P	=	pure
	c.	=	carrying
	d.	=	dilute (blue gene)
	BRN	=	brown
	BL	=	blue
	CH	=	chocolate
	LI	=	lilac
	X	=	mated to
	=	=	may produce

TABLE 1				
P.BRN	X	P.BRN	=	100% P.BRN.
P.BL	X	P.B.L.	=	100% P.BL.
P.CH.	X	P.CH	=	100% P.CH.
P.LI.	X	P.LI.	=	100% P.LI.
P.BRN	X	BRN.c.dil.	=	50% P.BRN, 50% BRN.c.dil.
BRN.c.dil.	X	BRN.c.dil.	=	25% P.BRN, 50% BRN.c.dil, 25% P.BL.
P.BRN	X	P.BL.	=	100% BRN.c.dil.
BRN.c.dil.	X	P.BL.	=	50% BRN.c.dil, 50% P.BL.
P.BRN.	X	P.CH.	=	100% BRN.c.CH.
BRN.c. CH.	X	P.CH.	=	50% BRN.c.CH, 50% P.CH.
BRN.c. CH	X	BRN.c.CH.	=	25% P.BRN, 50% BRN.c.CH, 25% P.CH.
P.CH.	X	P.LI.	=	100% CH.c.dil.
CH.c.dil.	X	P.LI.	=	50% CH.c.dil, 50% P.LI.
CH.c.dil	X	CH.c.dil.	=	25% P.CH, 50% CH.c.dil, 25% P.LI.

Of course, matings can be much more complex than the above once more than one gene is being carried, as in the case of a Brown Burmese carrying both chocolate and dilute. Such detail is outside the scope of this book, but the above matings give some idea of how colors in the group it has been recommended to start with are inherited. The basic ideas in the above have included:—

1. Chocolate can be carried by Brown and Blue.
2. Dilute can be carried by Brown or Chocolate.
3. Lilac is a combination of chocolate and the dilute gene.

The second group one might become interested in is the one which contains Reds, Creams and Tortoiseshells. As mentioned in Ch. 6, they are the sex-linked colors. The explanation of how the red group of colors is inherited is more complex and interested readers should again refer to a more detailed text on cat genetics. Despite this, one may progress to breeding in this group. The list in Table 2 below outlines the more simple matings and progeny likely:—

SYMBOLS USED: RD = Red
CRM = Cream
TOR = Tortoiseshell
M = Male
F = Female
Plus symbols used for Table 1.

TABLE 2:

P.RD	X P.RD	=	100% P.RD.
P.CRM	X P.CRM	=	100% P.CRM.
P.RD	X P.CRM	=	100% RD. c. dil (CRM).
RD.c.dil.	X P.CRM	=	50% Rd.c.dil, 50% P.CRM.
RD.c.dil.	X RD.c.dil	=	25% P.RD, 50% RD.c.dil, 25% P.CRM.
P.RD. M.	X TOR.F.	=	25% P.RD.M., 25% P.RD.F, 25% TOR.F, 25% BRN.M.
P.BRN.M.	X TOR.F.	=	25% BRN.M, 25% BRN.F, 25% TOR.F, 25% RD.M.

It needs to be understood that these are the very simplest of possible matings in this group. Once the dilute or the chocolate gene are added, the range of possible colors and colors being carried becomes considerably greater. Experience will teach the breeder what is possible, with the above giving a starting point. Most proposed matings could be calculated if the examples given in the two groups are combined in various ways.

In the future, new colors will be introduced into the Burmese range and color inheritance will become more complicated accordingly.

7. Exhibiting

The question of whether showing or breeding should come first is debatable. Whichever view is taken, quite clearly top quality stock is needed, as statistics show that most people who end up showing and/or breeding Burmese, start off with a pet which was bought just for company for the family. This makes perfect sense, as like any specialised field, most people know nothing initially about Burmese.

Very little grooming is required to keep your Burmese looking in the very best of health, like this Blue.

Whether one wants to breed Burmese or simply show occasionally, the show bench is the ideal place at which to see good Burmese. It gives one the opportunity to learn why some are sold as pets and others not.

If one is interested in showing Burmese, several shows should be visited to see how they are run, and what sort of cats win the major awards. Cats which conform as nearly as possible to the standard of the organization running the show, have bright clear eyes, good grooming and are pleasing to the eye, normally win. It is important to choose a cat with good temperament, as some felines become bored and upset at being shown regularly. Others quite enjoy the outings and really play to the public. These latter naturally win the personality section and also gain the eye of the judge when top awards are being considered, also judges can more readily assess the qualities of a well-behaved exhibit than an unruly one.

Burmese which win top prizes do not usually look much like the family pet. As even the best cats can produce pet kittens amongst their litter, the breeder has sold these former to be desexed without being used for breeding, with papers perhaps being available to the purchaser after proof of desexing is provided from a qualified veterinary surgeon. This protects the good name of the breeder, and prevents unwanted kittens from people not trained in the art of preventing a female from producing a family. It is equally probable that the same pet was sold on the condition that it not be shown; again to protect the breeder's reputation for quality.

Prices for kittens vary greatly from area to area within a country and even more so from country to country. Therefore it is virtually impossible to suggest what might be a fair price for a kitten. In any event, what may have seemed a high price for the first pet Burmese, will seem quite cheap to anyone who later buys a show cat. Pet kittens may only be a quarter of the price of a good show or breeding kitten, with kittens sold for breeding but not for showing perhaps a little cheaper. Factors like the show success of the breeder, his or her reputation and whether the kittens are from imported lines or lines with many champions on the pedigree all affect the price.

8. Burmese at a Glance

Country of origin	Uncertain.
Variety	Foreign Shorthair — modified foreign type.
Weight	Adult male: 8-10 lbs (4-5 kgs). Adult female: 6-8 lbs (3-4 kgs).
Longevity (av.)	Up to 12-15 years.
Number of teeth	Adults: 30
Earliest recommended breeding age	9 months both sexes.
Breeding season	Spring to autumn. No more than 2 litters per female per year.
Upper breeding age	Female: 8 years. Male 10 years.
Gestation period	63-65 days.
Litter size	Average 6, range commonly 4-8.
At birth	Average weight 3 oz. (50g.) Eyes closed. Born with short fur.
Eyes open	5-7 days, blue. Color changes later.
Weaning age	6 weeks. Milky foods at 3 weeks. Tinned foods from 4-6 weeks; 4 meals a day at 6-8 weeks (2 meat, 2 milk plus calcium & vitamins).
Food requirements	6 months — 3 meals daily (2 solid, 1 milk, 6-8 oz. meat daily). 9 months — 8 oz (225g.). meat daily, 2-3 meals daily. Adults — 8 oz (225g). meat daily, 1-2 meals daily. Always leave water to drink for all cats.
Coat color	Varies — about 10 colors currently bred.